Last summer my family stayed in a mobile
in Bettystown. It never rained at all,
so we were outside the whole time,
on the beach.

CHRISTINE'S HOLIDAY

The beach was
packed down the
bottom end but we
were at the top end.

I can swim kinda
with arm-bands.
We got loads of
shells as well.

We found a green shell.
We went to the amusements as well.

I nearly lost all my money on the slot
machines but I won some back as well.
Enough to buy my duck soap, but I'm
never going to use it.

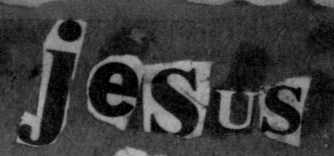

NORMAN'S STORY

I came from Nigeria

five years ago.

I came to Drogheda

because I liked it.

I have an **angel** in

my box because an angel

came with me

on the plane.

Jesus created the angels

and that's why

He is in my box too.

DAIRE'S TRAIN JOURNEY

This is my journey.

I went from Galway
to Belfast by train.

I saw a boat in
the sea.

I stopped off at a
shop and got sweets.

My sister was sick
and couldn't go,
but she went to the
cinema instead.

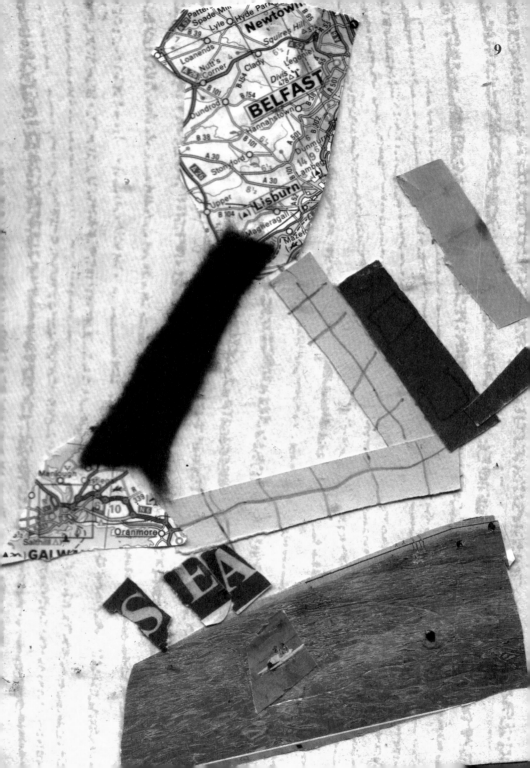

I'll never forget Blackpool,

I went when I was six with my

grandparents and uncle Sean.

We used to go on all the rides and

spend lots of money on the

amusements.

Every night we went to the disco

and have mad crack until

half four in the morning.

My journey was the best journey ever,

but it's a long time ago.

But we liked it so much we're going back again.

I bet it'll be all changed round,

but I hope the rides are the same.

RACHEL'S TRIP TO BLACKPOOL

My ears popped on
the plane,
and I *hated* that.
I didn't like
the food either.
When I went down to
the pool my brother
nearly drowned me.
My mum and
sister *jumped in*
and saved me.

I loved the shopping and the Russian dolls you see

in the box.

There were hOOps hanging over the pool you could play with.

AINE'S TRIP TO TURKEY

Bettystown is class.

I love the money machines.

I hit them a kick and the money falls out.

But the sea

BILLY IN BETTYSTOWN.

is the best part.

I love swimming.

I have great fun with my family.

I bought the man in my box in Bettystown with the old money.

My Uncle was going to get
married in Pakistan.

We went to the wedding from
Ireland.

It took two days in the
aeroplane over the sea.

The woman was wearing four
or five rings.

We had chicken and rice and
special food.

IBRAHIM'S
WEDDING
JOURNEY

I played with my
cousins and friends.

I was happy and sad when we
were leaving.

married

My name is Laurynas. I came from Lithuania by bus. I saw soldiers and an aeroplane when I was leaving. In Lithuania I lived in a house with five storeys. When we had to go my mother bought the tickets. The journey was good because I liked the tea and coffee on the bus. It took three days to get to Ireland.

LAURYNAS'S JOURNEY FROM LITHUANIA

In January we left South Africa.

My Dad wanted to get more money.

Dad got the tickets and we went to

the airport. The weather was

always sunny in South Africa,

and in Drogheda it was raining.

I had one birthday in Ireland.

The South African flag is black,

green, blue red and white.

I miss South Africa and my cousins.

Some of my cousin's are in England. Something I like about Ireland is the T.V. It rains so much you have to stay inside.

MICHAEL'S JOURNEY

MARTIN'S
TRIP

I went to Bettystown beach and there was lots to do. I went swimming, built sand castles, looked for crabs. I bought water balloons and threw them at Connor. The best bit was eating ice-cream.

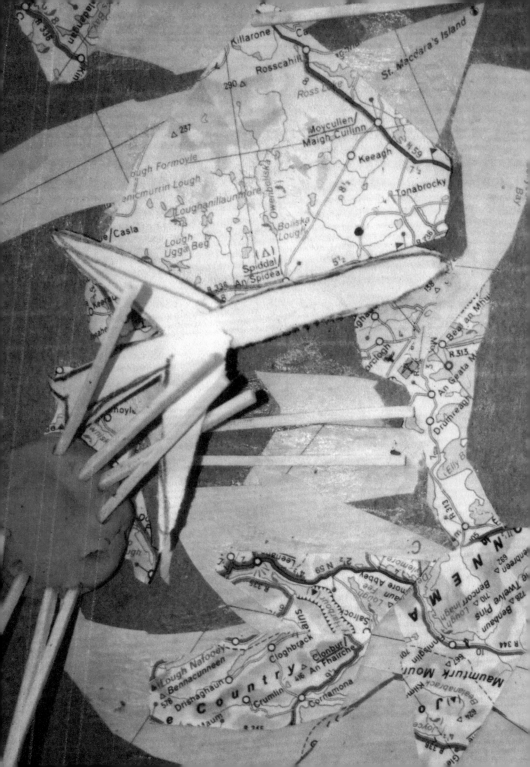

irde/Height/Taille (12)

168 cm

SAAD'S STORY

When I went to Disneyland I had lots of fun.

My sisters came with me on the swings.

We met Goofy and took a picture.

I had a ride on the cars.

I went to Pakistan on an aeroplane.

I had lots of fun with my cousins and friends.

In Islamabad I met my Granddad and Grandma.

They were so happy to see me again.

They hugged me and I hugged them.

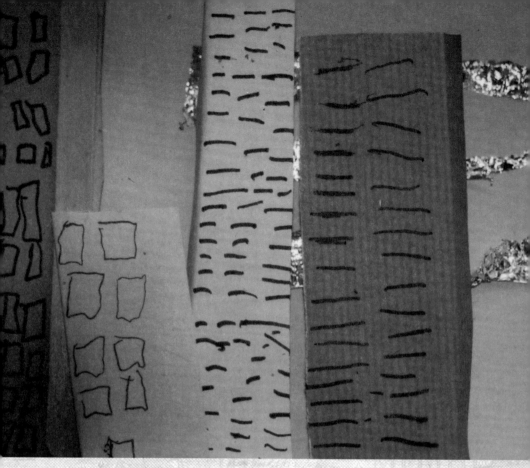

My family went to New York for
Christmas in 2000.
The Twin Towers were still there then.
From the top everything looked tiny.
I felt big.
There were tons of people in the streets.
We got lots of limousines on video.
We stayed in an apartment where the rooms
were underground.
They were nice and tidy but a bit dark.

**GERARD'S TRIP
TO NEW YORK**

ANOTHER NEW YORK STORY

Last year we went to New York.
It was roasting even when it was raining it
was still hot.
I jumped in a swimming pool the first day I
got there. I didn't know it was the deep end
and I nearly drowned. Some girl saved me.

People say New York is violent but I got a
beating in Dundalk over a mobile phone. The
best bit of New York was the arcades. I had
french toast and banana milkshakes for
breakfast every day.

Fishing is the best thing about Offaly. We caught three fish in the canal. But you can't eat them, they're too small. Afterwards I went to my cousin's party. She turned nine.

HAMILTON'S TRIP TO OFFALY

I moved to Dundalk
when I was three so I
don't remember much
about Laoise.
All I remember from
that age is Junior
Infants with my brother.
The most travelling we
do now is go to Offaly
when we have days off.
Our house is near the
gaelic pitch and I love
watching the games.

I spent three weeks visiting Chicago, Ohio and Canada. There's a big difference between the U.S.A. and Canada. Canada smells more like the sea with Niagara Falls so near. The Falls sound like a load of trucks going past you. There was a big adventure fair besides the Falls.

I'd love to go back.

LEAH'S NORTH AMERICAN TRIP

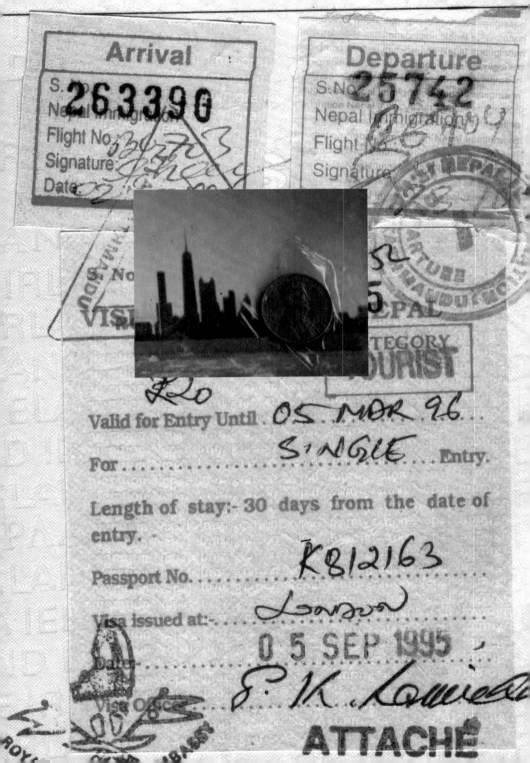

Arrival
S. No. **263390**
Nepal Immigration
Flight No: 307703
Signature:
Date:

Departure
S.No. **25742**
Nepal Immigration
Flight No.
Signature:

VIS...

TEGORY
OURIST

£20

Valid for Entry Until .. O5. MAR 96...

For.................................. SINGLE .... Entry.

Length of stay:- 30 days from the date of entry. -

Passport No............. K812163

Visa issued at:-..............London

Date................ 0 5 SEP 1995

Visa Office.........

ATTACHÉ

I have friends in Cork and we went there on a journey by car.

When I was in my friend's house, my brother pushed me down the stairs and I nearly broke my leg.

My leg was very sore and I had to go to the doctor.

Next day I went to the beach and a model train shop.

I bought things there.

We stayed up very late.

BRENDAN'S CORK TRIP

I went to see my cousin's and spend a couple of weeks with them. I hardly ever see them and some of them are my favourites. I go to see Alisha and Grace play gaelic.

I never go to school when I'm in Offaly and I go to bed at midnight. I don't have to clean up there and my Aunty has the breakfast on the table. A fry.

JOSHUA'S TRIP TO OFFALY

My journey is about Africa and Ireland.

I was living in Africa but I came to Ireland in 2002.

Africa has loads of gold.

MAXWELL'S STORY

Everyday you can find gold there.

Some people bring the gold to Ireland.

Ireland is a good country because it has good teachers.

It also has a lot of rain, not like Africa.

Africa is sunny.

That's all.

When I travelled to the pool and I was about to jump in, I remembered I still had my shoes on. My shoes were very wet after.

I dived in and started playing football with my friends.

My mum and dad were sitting in the shallow bit.

Then we dived in again. I had to go home in my bare feet.

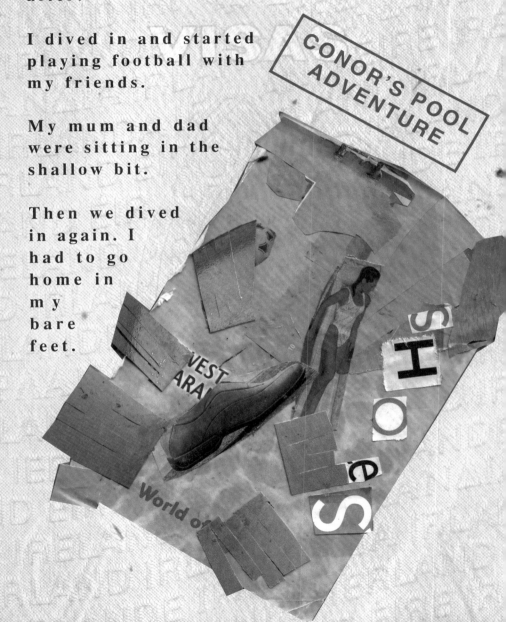

CONOR'S POOL ADVENTURE

When I am big I
am going to have
a ballO On race
with my friend
Ibrahim
a c r o s s
Pakistan.

saad's journey

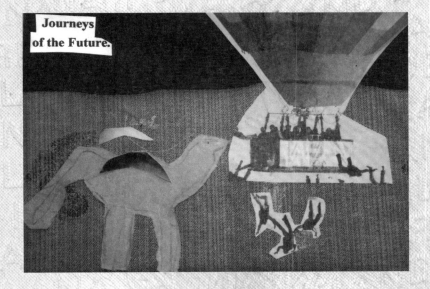

Journeys of the Future.

I want to visit
Paris and go up
the Eiffel tower

PARIS

I liked going swimming and playing tennis.

I pushed a girl into the pool because she was
annoying me.

That night I had to buy her two packets of
sweets to make up.

I slept in a mobile home
for the week.

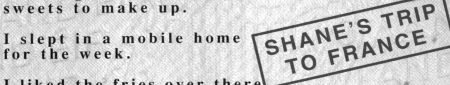

SHANE'S TRIP
TO FRANCE

I liked the fries over there

My house of the
future is in Ireland. I
want to bring my
friends there.

MAXWELL

I want to go to Portugal
where the sun is bright
and the sea is cold.
I want to be good-looking,
happy and have a car.
I might take my teacher
and Maxwell to Portugal.

DAIRE

BRAZIL

My future journey is to Brazil, because of the famous footballers. I would like to go there with my family. It would be fun.

BILLY

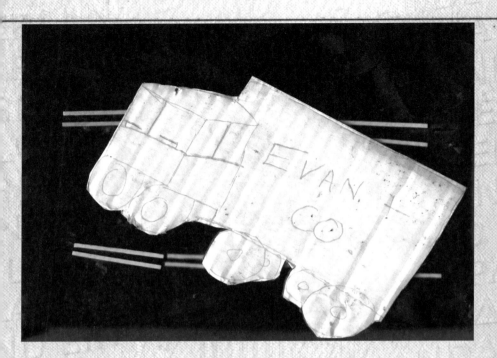

When I grow up I want to work with the corporation and drive the lorries and vans. I want a van of my own and my own house. All my friends can come over, even the teacher.

EVAN

I'd like to discover Ireland by camper van. I'd like to meet people who speak Irish. Someday I'd like to speak Irish.

All around the world. I want to go all around the world to see different countries like Italy, France, Spain, Portugal and America, Germany (and Offaly of course.)

JOSHUA

In the holidays my mother and I are going to Dublin. We will go to a match to see Liverpool play.
Then we will go for a
trip on the river in a boat.

LAURYNAS

ADRIAN'S WEDDING

I went to Limerick a year ago cos of a wedding. Me Uncle was getting married. We went in a car but I didn't like it. I knew I was going to get sick. And I did. Then I had to travel the whole way back. When you travel sit in the front and look at the cars and then you won't get sick.

The angels are in
heaven. Tell you
what Jesus is in
there with them.

When I'm dead
the angels will
take me there.

NORMAN

In the future I will go around the world by plane. I'd rather go in a plane than anything else. I'd like to go with my wee niece. We'll be away for two years. We'll have to save up all our wages. I really want to meet people in other countries and learn new languages.

NICOLE

When I am 12
I want to go underwater

and see the sea monsters
chasing me.

I want to see fish swimming
around our watership.

DAVID

This is a map of the world.
Ireland is one small country.
But many children travel to other
countries and children come here from
all over the world.
This is why our book is called

Travellers of the World.

The End

We hope you enjoyed reading
about our travels.

What we found out making this book,
is that all children love travelling.

Bon Voyage!